Teaching and Learning
Key Stage 2
Sentence Resource Pack

Louis Fidge

Literacy   Year 5

Sentence Year 5

First published 2001

Letts Educational,
The Chiswick Centre, 414 Chiswick High Rd
London W4 5TF

Tel 020 8996 3333
Fax 020 8742 8390
www.letts-education.com

Illustrations © Phil Burrows, Richard Duszsczak, Simon Girling &
Associates (Liz Sawyer), John Plumb, Sylvie Poggio Artists Agency
(Simon Jacobs) and Ken Vail Graphic Design (Liz Bryan)

Designed, edited and produced by Gecko Ltd.

British Library Cataloguing-in-Publication Data
A CIP record for this book is available from the British Library.

ISBN: 1 84085 6130

Printed in the UK.

Every effort has been made to trace copyright holders and to obtain
their permission for the use of copyright material. The authors and
publishers would gladly receive information enabling them to rectify
an error or omission in subsequent editions.

Letts Educational Ltd, a division of Granada Learning Ltd. Part of the
Granada Media Group.

Contents

Overview of Letts Sentence Level copymasters

Letts Sentence Level copymasters:

- provide opportunities for the systematic introduction, teaching, consolidation and development of grammar and punctuation
- may be used independently or alongside any other materials being used
- are designed in a structured and accessible way
- incorporate a variety of clearly focused activities, providing for both differentiation and development
- provide opportunities for class, group and individual work
- may also usefully be used as homework assignments
- are appealing and child-friendly, and engage the learner in meaningful ways
- cover the requirements in UK and Republic of Ireland curriculum documents and the National Literacy Framework
- provide a photocopiable bank of resource material which is flexible and easy to use, and ideal for the busy teacher

Using the copymasters

The copymasters may be used with the whole class, with a group or individually, as appropriate. They may be used to introduce or follow-up the teaching of any specific grammar or punctuation concept. In whatever context they are used, it is essential that the tasks are discussed with the children, so that the teaching point is made clear and the children understand exactly what they have to do.

There are *three* copymasters (numbered 1–3) for *each* objective. The learning objective is always clearly stated at the bottom of each sheet. Each sheet begins with a 'Remember' box which introduces the concept being taught, provides key vocabulary and gives an example. This is then followed by the main activity.

The *first* copymaster is always fairly straightforward, with a strong practice element. Instructional language is kept deliberately simple.

The *second* and *third* copymasters in each set extend and develop the concept being taught, offering differentiation in terms of increased levels of difficulty.

Scope and sequence of the Word Sentence Level copymasters

Year 5/P6

Unit title	Objective
Essential words	to investigate which words are essential to meaning
Changing the order – not meaning	to change the order of words within a sentence without changing the meaning
Subject and verb agreement	to explore the need for agreement between nouns and verbs in sentences
Standard English	to practise using some of the conventions of Standard English
Double negatives	to avoid the use of double negatives
Making longer sentences	to practise creating more complex sentences
Direct speech	to understand how dialogue is set out and punctuated
Reported speech	to understand the difference between direct and reported speech
Thinking about punctuation – commas	to use punctuation to aid the reader
Verb tenses (past, present)	to revise work on past and present verb tenses
Verb tenses (past, present, future)	to revise work on past, present and future verb tenses
Auxiliary verbs	to investigate the use of auxiliary verbs
Verb forms	to focus on different verb forms
Verbs – 1st, 2nd, 3rd person	to investigate the use of the 1st, 2nd and 3rd person
Common and proper nouns	to revise common and proper nouns
Concrete and abstract nouns	to explore concrete and abstract nouns
Pronouns	to revise some of the functions of pronouns
Homonyms	to explore homonyms and ambiguity
Ambiguity	to explore ambiguity
Summarising	to construct texts in different ways without losing their meaning
Using fewer words	to discover how substituting words may affect the meaning of sentences
Experimenting with words	to discover how substituting words may affect the meaning of sentences
Prepositions	to understand the function of prepositions
Speaking and writing	to explore some of the differences between spoken and written English
Apostrophes showing ownership	to revise the use of apostrophes to show ownership
Clauses	to investigate clauses
More about clauses	to investigate clauses further
Connectives	to use connectives to join clauses together
Punctuation and meaning	to use punctuation accurately to aid the reader
A sense of audience	to understand how writing can be adapted for different audiences and purposes

Name _____   Date _____

Essential words (1)

Work out which verb is missing from each sentence.
Write each sentence correctly.

mowed	stopped	turned	flew	roared
sped	knocked	grabbed	started	ran

1 The sports car round the corner.

   The sports car sped round the corner

2 The lion loudly.

   _____

3 The bus at the bus stop.

   _____

4 The bird out of the tree.

   _____

5 The programme at nine o'clock.

   _____

6 Tom on the television.

   _____

7 The lady on the door.

   _____

8 The silly boy across the busy road.

   _____

9 The man the lawn.

   _____

10 The thief the lady's handbag.

   _____

Objective: to investigate which words are essential to meaning

Essential words (2)

Remember

Some words are **essential to meaning** e.g. A **noun** in this sentence is missing — 'The (dog) ate its dinner.'

These sentences do not make sense because each one has a noun missing. Think of a suitable noun and rewrite each sentence correctly.

1 The old was falling down.

_____

2 Out of the cave came a fierce.

_____

3 The girl hid behind the.

_____

4 The crept slowly towards the birds.

_____

5 I turned off the and went to sleep.

_____

6 The boy got muddy when he fell in a.

_____

7 The blasted off from the launch pad.

_____

8 The lived in the wood.

_____

9 The girl wore her best to go to the party.

_____

10 The angry stormed out of the shop.

_____

Objective: to investigate which words are essential to meaning

Essential words (3)

Remember

Some words are **essential to meaning** e.g. A **noun** in this sentence is missing – 'The (dog) ate its dinner.' This time, the **verb** is missed out – 'The dog (ate) its dinner.'

Each sentence has a word missing.
Think of a sensible word to complete each sentence.
Rewrite each sentence.
Say whether the missing word is a noun (N) or a verb (V).
The first sentence has been done for you.

(1) The referee the whistle loudly.

The referee _blew_ the whistle loudly. (V)

(2) I made myself a jam.

_____

(3) I the water with one gulp.

_____

(4) The boy dived into the.

_____

(5) The helicopter over the house.

_____

(6) I planted some in the garden.

_____

(7) The greedy boy all his money on sweets.

_____

(8) The came to see me when I was ill.

_____

(9) The lumberjack the tree down with an axe.

_____

(10) How many are left in the box?

_____

Objective: to investigate which words are essential to meaning

Changing the order – not the meaning (1)

Remember

Sometimes we can **change the order of words** within a sentence, **without changing the meaning** e.g. 'I ran home quickly.'
'Quickly I ran home.'

Underline the adverb in each sentence.
Rewrite each sentence and begin it with the adverb.
The first has been done for you.

(1) The knight faced the dragon <u>bravely</u>.

   <u>Bravely the knight faced the dragon.</u>

(2) The footballer passed the ball skilfully.

_____

(3) The children crept quietly out of the room.

_____

(4) The child stroked the cat gently.

_____

(5) The boy accepted his prize proudly.

_____

(6) I read my book slowly.

_____

(7) The car stopped suddenly.

_____

(8) I slammed the door noisily.

_____

(9) The sun shone brightly in the sky.

_____

(10) The old man sat down tiredly.

_____

Objective: to change the order of words within a sentence without changing the meaning

Changing the order – not the meaning (2)

Remember

Sometimes we can **change the order of words** within a sentence, **without changing the meaning** e.g. 'I ran home quickly.' 'Quickly I ran home.'

The reporting clause comes at the end of each of these sentences and is underlined. Rewrite each sentence and begin it with the reporting clause. Punctuate the sentences correctly!

1 "Tell me where you've hidden the treasure," <u>the pirate demanded</u>.

The pirate demanded, "Tell me where you've hidden the treasure."

2 "That's not fair!" <u>the children complained</u>.

_____

3 "I'm going shopping," <u>Mrs Shah called.</u>

_____

4 "My garden needs digging," <u>the man said</u>.

_____

5 "How far away is Dublin?" <u>Tom asked</u>.

_____

6 "I want something to eat," <u>Edward moaned</u>.

_____

7 "Have you seen my shoes?" <u>Shannon enquired</u>.

_____

8 "I feel sick," <u>Sacha groaned</u>.

_____

9 "Bring me my lunch!" <u>the king roared</u>.

_____

10 "Tom is so handsome!" <u>Sarah sighed</u>.

_____

Objective: to change the order of words within a sentence without changing the meaning

Changing the order – not the meaning (3)

Sometimes we can **change the order of words** within a sentence, **without changing the meaning** e.g. 'I ran home after school.'
'After school, I ran home.'

Choose the best phrase to complete each sentence.
Then write each sentence again, this time beginning with the phrase.

through the woods	after the storm	many years ago	in bed
in the distance	from the greengrocer	into the pond	on the seashore

(1) The children looked for shells <u>on the seashore</u>.

    On the seashore the children looked for shells.

(2) We could just see a ship approaching _____

_____

(3) I splashed in the puddles _____

_____

(4) I bought some fruit _____

_____

(5) The frog hopped _____

_____

(6) The owl flew silently _____

_____

(7) Dinosaurs lived _____

_____

(8) James read his book _____

_____

Objective: to change the order of words within a sentence without changing the meaning

Subject and verb agreement (1)

Remember

Every sentence must have a **subject** (the main person or thing it is about) and a **verb**. The subject and verb must **agree** e.g. 'The children *were* happy.' not 'The children *was* happy.'

Rewrite each sentence. Choose the correct form of the verb.

1 It (is/are) snowing.

_____

2 Some birds (is/are) singing in the trees.

_____

3 The elephant (was/were) bathing in the river.

_____

4 We (was/were) late for school.

_____

5 The crocodile (is/are) sleeping under a tree.

_____

6 What (is/are) you good at doing?

_____

7 (Is/Are) it a long way to go?

_____

8 (Is/Are) the insects annoying you?

_____

9 The bees (was/were) buzzing around the flowers.

_____

10 Once upon a time there (was/were) an ugly giant.

_____

Objective: to explore the need for agreement between nouns and verbs in sentences

Subject and verb agreement (2)

Remember

Every sentence must have a **subject** (the main person or thing it is about) and a **verb**. The subject and verb must **agree** e.g. 'The children *were* happy.' not 'The children *was* happy.'

Rewrite each sentence. Choose the correct form of the verb.

(1) The children often (swim/swims) in the sea.

_____

(2) Tom (bring/brought) his new computer game for us to see.

_____

(3) My uncle usually (go/goes) away each weekend.

_____

(4) I (did/done) my homework last night.

_____

(5) They (has/have) some very good books at the library.

_____

(6) Our teacher (give/gave) us a spelling test.

_____

(7) Sarah (has/have) a lot of homework to do.

_____

(8) Who (write/wrote) you that letter?

_____

(9) I (sees/saw) a scary film last night.

_____

(10) We (has/have) been playing tennis.

_____

Objective: to explore the need for agreement between nouns and verbs in sentences

Subject and verb agreement (3)

Every sentence must have a **subject** (the main person or thing it is about) and a **verb**. The subject and verb must **agree** e.g. 'The children *were* happy.' not 'The children *was* happy.'

Rewrite each sentence correctly.

1 Last week I <u>seen</u> the a good programme on television.

_____

2 When we were late we <u>run</u> all the way to school.

_____

3 Everyone <u>goes</u> very quiet when the teacher came in.

_____

4 Neither of the boys <u>comed</u> home in time for tea.

_____

5 I <u>done</u> all my maths correctly.

_____

6 None of the kittens <u>were</u> asleep.

_____

7 <u>Was</u> either of you right?

_____

8 I <u>has</u> been to the cinema.

_____

9 They all <u>gived</u> some money towards the cost of the trip.

_____

10 Only a few of the children <u>bringed</u> any food with them.

_____

Objective: to explore the need for agreement between nouns and verbs in sentences

Name _____   Date _____

Standard English (1)

Remember

Standard English is the kind of language you are expected to use in school e.g. 'Anna and I went home.' (*not* 'Me and Anna went home.')

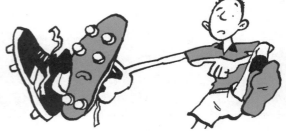

Cut out the sentences in Standard and non-standard English and match them up.

Non-standard English

These ain't my boots.	We done it yesterday.
All of us was hungry.	Me and Tom went home.
Me socks was in me bag.	What yer want?
I'm gonna play outside.	I saw the man what done it.
That's real naughty.	I could of eaten it.

Standard English

I'm going to play outside.	We did it yesterday.
That's really naughty.	My socks were in my bag.
Tom and I went home.	What do you want?
I saw the man who did it.	These are not my boots.
All of us were hungry.	I could have eaten it.

Objective: to practise using some of the conventions of Standard English

Standard English (2)

Remember

Standard English is the kind of language you are expected to use in school e.g. 'Anna and I went home.' (*not* 'Me and Anna went home.')

Rewrite these non-standard English sentences in Standard English.

1. You should of took more care.

2. My mum learnt me how to swim.

3. Give me one of them apples.

4. Who's got me book?

5. It ain't fair!

6. I wanna go home.

7. I can run more faster than you.

8. We seen him do it.

1 _____

2 _____

3 _____

4 _____

5 _____

6 _____

7 _____

8 _____

Objective: to practise using some of the conventions of Standard English

Standard English (3)

Standard English is the kind of language you are expected to use in school e.g. 'Anna and I went home.' (*not* 'Me and Anna went home.')

This short story has lots of examples of non-standard English in it. Rewrite it in Standard English. Continue on the other side of this sheet if necessary.

When Mrs Smith saw Amy she were surprised.

"What you bin doin'?" she shouted.

"Me and Emma was in the park when we seed a space ship land. Lots of little aliens come out of it. They was all green," Amy answered. "We ran 'ome as quick as we could."

"I s'pose that's how your new trainers what I give you is all muddy!" Mrs Smith cried. "You ain't gonna get any more."

"That ain't fair!" Emma said. "It weren't my fault."

"Don't tell me no lies! I bet there wasn't any aliens at all," Mrs Smith shouted.

Just then, a strange-looking green hand opened the door...

Objective: to practise using some of the conventions of Standard English

Double negatives (1)

Negative means '**no**'. It is **incorrect** to use a **double negative** in the **same** sentence e.g. 'I never saw nothing.' ☒
'I never saw anything.' ☑

Match up the sentences containing a single and a double negative.
On another piece of paper copy down the correct form of each sentence.

There isn't no point in crying.	He wasn't anywhere near me.
I don't want no sweets.	The man didn't say anything.
He wasn't nowhere near me.	There isn't any point in crying.
I don't eat no biscuits.	A cat hasn't got any wings.
A cat hasn't got no wings.	I don't want any sweets.
The man didn't say nothing.	The girl never saw anybody.
I never did nothing wrong.	I didn't eat any biscuits.
The girl never saw nobody.	I never did anything wrong.

Objective: to avoid the use of double negatives

Double negatives (2)

Remember

Negative means '**no**'. It is **incorrect** to use a **double negative** in the **same** sentence e.g. 'I never saw nothing.' ☒ 'I never saw anything.' ☑

Cut out these sentences. Sort them into two sets – those which contain a single negative and those which contain a double negative. (There will be eight in each set.)

That is not right.	I haven't got no football boots.
I can't do anything.	The girl didn't say nothing.
I never saw nobody.	I have not seen anyone.
I have not been anywhere.	I didn't go nowhere nice.
He don't know nothing.	I haven't got any money.
I don't want no trouble.	They weren't anywhere near the shop.
I'm never going swimming again.	The children did not take no notice.
He couldn't find his sister nowhere.	I haven't done anything wrong.

Objective: to avoid the use of double negatives

Double negatives (3)

Remember

Negative means 'no'. It is **incorrect** to use a **double negative** in the **same** sentence e.g. 'I never saw nothing.' ☒
'I never saw anything.' ✔

Write each sentence in correct standard English.

(1) I couldn't find my slippers nowhere.

_____

(2) I haven't never been abroad.

_____

(3) I never went nowhere during the holidays.

_____

(4) We haven't got no money.

_____

(5) She don't go swimming no more.

_____

(6) I'm not never going in that cave again.

_____

(7) She doesn't know nothing.

_____

(8) I don't want no help with my homework.

_____

(9) I don't like nobody next door.

_____

(10) When it was time to clear up, Tom wasn't nowhere to be seen.

_____

Objective: to avoid the use of double negatives

Making longer sentences (1)

Remember

We use **conjunctions** (or **connectives**) to **join** two or more **sentences** together to make one longer sentence e.g. I had a drink (*because*) I was thirsty.

Use the conjunction 'because' to join these pairs of sentences. Write them as one long sentence. The first has been done for you.

1. Sam was allowed to stay up late. It was his birthday.

   Sam was allowed to stay up late because it was his birthday.

2. Everybody liked Mr Charles. He was always happy.

   _____

3. Emma did not go to the party. She had not been invited.

   _____

4. Ali won the painting competition. He tried his very best.

   _____

5. There was a traffic jam on the motorway. There had been an accident.

   _____

6. I am going out to play. I am fed up.

   _____

7. I am very cold. It is snowing outside.

   _____

8. Go to bed early. Tomorrow we must get up before dawn.

   _____

9. The bird flew into the bird-house. It was building a nest there.

   _____

10. I wrote a letter to my aunt. She sent me a present.

    _____

Objective: to practise creating more complex sentences

Name _____ Date _____

Making longer sentences (2)

Match up the pairs of sentences that go together.
Choose 'although' or 'as' to join these pairs of sentences.
Write each pair as one long sentence on another sheet of paper.
Do it like this:
The footballer headed the ball as the referee blew his whistle.

The footballer headed the ball.	He was sitting on the train.
Ben did not eat his dinner.	My teacher was calling the register.
We managed to reach the island.	Her mum had told her not to.
Mr Smith read the newspaper.	The referee blew his whistle.
I arrived at school.	He was very hungry.
The police hurried to the scene.	I was walking down the road.
Emma went out.	It was a long way away.
I met my friend.	They were too late to catch the robber.

Objective: to practise creating more complex sentences

Making longer sentences (3)

Remember

We use **conjunctions** (or **connectives**) to **join** two or more **sentences** together to make one longer sentence e.g. I had a drink (*because*) I was thirsty.

Rewrite these pairs of sentences. Make them into one long sentence. Use 'as', 'because' or 'although' at the **beginning** of the sentence.

(1) I sheltered under a tree. The rain began to fall.

As the rain began to fall, I sheltered under a tree.

(2) Jack hurried home. He wanted to play on the computer.

_____

(3) I walked along the street. I saw a lovely pair of trainers in the shoe shop.

_____

(4) His tea was ready. Tom was too excited to eat.

_____

(5) Sam was not allowed to go out. He had disobeyed the teacher.

_____

(6) The sun was setting. The plane touched down.

_____

(7) The moon is millions of miles away. It seems very near.

_____

(8) Ben was strong. He was small.

_____

(9) I ate a bag of crisps. I watched the television.

_____

(10) I put on some dark glasses. The sun was too bright.

_____

Objective: to practise creating more complex sentences

Direct speech (1)

Remember

When we write down the **direct speech** of someone, we put the words they actually say inside **speech marks**. e.g. "What's the weather like?" Sarah asked.

Copy these sentences containing direct speech. Put in the missing speech marks correctly.

1 The magician said, Abracadabra!

_____

2 I hate cabbage! Amy exclaimed.

_____

3 Pass me my pen, please, William said.

_____

4 Kyle asked, What is the date today?

_____

5 It's lovely and warm in the water, Shannon shouted.

_____

6 Let's play on the computer, suggested Paul.

_____

7 Read me a story, the child pleaded.

_____

8 Stop making so much noise, the teacher ordered.

_____

9 The giant exclaimed, I'm hungry.

_____

10 Which way is it to the shops? the stranger asked.

_____

Objective: to understand how dialogue is set out and punctuated

Direct speech (2)

When we write down the **direct speech** of someone, we put the words they actually say inside **speech marks**. e.g. "What's the weather like?" Sarah asked.

Put in the missing speech marks in each sentence.
Then write each sentence in a different way.
The first is done for you.

1 The girl said, "I can stand on my head."

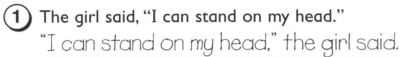
"I can stand on my head," the girl said.

2 I can swim further than you, the boy boasted.

_____

3 The traffic warden explained, You can't park here, I'm afraid.

_____

4 I feel too hungry, Dionne complained.

_____

5 James asked, What team do you support?

_____

6 Stop cheating! shouted Cara.

_____

7 Emma asked, Has anyone borrowed my felt-tip pens?

_____

8 Get me my tea! the duke ordered.

_____

9 The small girl said, I'm going to the seaside tomorrow.

_____

10 The reporter explained, The fire started on the ground floor.

_____

Objective: to understand how dialogue is set out and punctuated

Direct speech (3)

When we write down the **direct speech** of someone, we put the words they actually say inside **speech marks**. e.g. "What's the weather like?" Sarah asked. Remember to **start a new line** whenever a **different person** begins to speak.

Rewrite the following passage in direct speech.
Start a new line for each new speaker.
Punctuate the sentences correctly.

Where are you going with that ball my mum asked I'm going into the garden I replied What are you going to do she asked I'm going to practise heading the ball against the wall I answered But the garden's too small my mum exclaimed Don't worry I'll be careful I assured her Make sure you don't head the ball near the windows my mother warned I won't I replied with a grin

Continue the story on the other side of the sheet. Include lots of dialogue.

Objective: to understand how dialogue is set out and punctuated

Reported speech (1)

Cut out these sentences.
Match up each sentence in Set A in direct speech,
with the same sentence in Set B, in reported speech.

Set A – sentences in direct speech

"What's the matter, Tom?" the teacher asked.

"Stop shouting, James," Mrs Bennet ordered.

"I've won the lottery!" Mr Batram exclaimed.

"When is your birthday?" the man asked William.

"Has anyone seen my coat?" the lady asked.

"Help!" shouted the drowning man.

Set B – sentences in reported speech

Mr Bartram exclaimed that he had won the lottery.

The teacher asked Tom what was the matter.

The drowning man shouted for help.

The man asked William when his birthday was.

Mrs Bennett told James to stop shouting.

The lady asked if anyone had seen her coat.

Objective: to understand the difference between direct and reported speech

Reported speech (2)

Remember

"I like sweets," the girl said. (**direct** speech)
The girl said that she liked sweets. (**reported** speech)
In reported speech: a) **no speech marks** are used; b) the speaker's **exact** words are **not** used; c) the **tense** of the **verbs** has been **changed**.

Cut out these sentences.
Divide them into two sets:
a) sentences containing direct speech
b) sentences containing reported speech.
There will be six sentences in each set.

- ✂

"I want an apple," said Anna.

James said that he had finished his book.

Paul said that he watched a good film last night.

"What have you lost?" asked Sarah.

"You need a new tyre," Mr Brown explained.

Tom said that the grass was very long.

Amy asked if she could stay up late.

The dentist said, "You need a filling."

Mrs Smith told the children to be quiet.

The lady said that she was pleased she had come.

"I don't know how to use the computer," the old man said.

Mr Shah said, "It's my birthday today."

Objective: to understand the difference between direct and reported speech

Reported speech (3)

"I like sweets," the girl said.
(**direct** speech)
The girl said that she liked sweets.
(**reported** speech)
In reported speech: a) **no speech marks** are used; b) the speaker's **exact** words are **not** used;
c) the **tense** of the **verbs** is sometimes **changed**.

Rewrite each of the sentences below in reported speech.

(1) "I've been stung!" the lady shrieked.

_____

(2) "I've lost my lunch box," Shaun said.

_____

(3) "Stop cheating, Sarah!" Mrs Davis ordered.

_____

(4) "Come here, Wags!" Mr Abrahams shouted to his dog.

_____

(5) "I'm one hundred years old," Mrs Hambrook remarked.

_____

(6) "I know how to mend a puncture," boasted Rachel.

_____

(7) "Will you help me with my spellings?" Zoe asked Amelia.

_____

(8) "Where do you want me to plant this tree?" the man asked his wife.

_____

(9) "My Mum has dyed her hair," James told Samantha.

_____

(10) "Why did you do it?" the policewoman asked the shoplifter.

_____

Objective: to understand the difference between direct and reported speech

Thinking about punctuation – commas (1)

Remember

We use **punctuation marks** to **help the reader make sense** of what they are reading. We use **commas** to **separate extra bits** that are added to the **beginning** or **ending** of sentences e.g. Pass my slippers, please.

Rewrite each sentence. Put in the missing comma that separates the bit that has been added to the beginning or end of each sentence.

1 What are you doing Paul?

_____

2 Have you seen my bag Emma?

_____

3 Sorry sir.

_____

4 Give it to me please.

_____

5 I can do it I think.

_____

6 You're wrong aren't you?

_____

7 We'll go tomorrow shall we?

_____

8 I would like a cake a doughnut.

_____

9 Dear me I'm lost!

_____

10 It's mine I'm sure.

_____

11 Yes that's my book.

_____

12 Good gracious it's a monster!

_____

Objective: to use punctuation to aid the reader

Thinking about punctuation – commas (2)

Remember

We use **punctuation marks** to **help the reader make sense** of what they are reading. **Commas** help to **break up** longer sentences into **smaller parts** e.g. When they went out in the car, Emma's father asked her to shut the window.

Join up the beginning and ending of each sentence.
Write the sentences you make on a separate piece of paper.
Each sentence has a comma missing. Remember to put it in.

(1) When I was a baby   I watch my favourite pop group.

(2) As soon as the rain stopped   I brushed my teeth.

(3) Whenever they are on TV   I could not walk.

(4) I ate the cake   I got undressed.

(5) After I had washed my face   I went out.

(6) Before I had a bath even though   I wasn't hungry.

(7) If my mum is happy   my teacher was pleased.

(8) As my work was so neat   she sings while she is working.

(9) Since sweets contain sugar   I will not pass my exam.

(10) Unless I work hard   you should not eat too many of them.

Objective: to use punctuation to aid the reader

Thinking about punctuation – commas (3)

We use **punctuation marks** to **help the reader make sense** of what they are reading. Commas are often used to **separate off phrases** in sentences which make them more interesting e.g. Sarah, the best swimmer in the class, can swim over one kilometre.

Rewrite each sentence.
Choose a suitable phrase from the box
to put in it to make it more interesting.
Don't forget to use commas.

trembling with fear	all rusty and dented	my fluffy white rabbit
the great explorer	snarling and barking	dark and menacing
fat and green	the tall oak tree	glinting in the sun

1 Snowy lives in a hutch.

_____

2 Sir Walter Raleigh returned home after a long sea voyage.

_____

3 I hid behind the door when I saw the ghost.

_____

4 The frog jumped out of the pond.

_____

5 Mr Smith's car clattered down the street.

_____

6 The volcano erupted without warning.

_____

7 I climbed the tree which stood at the bottom of the garden.

_____

8 The dog chased the burglar.

_____

9 The jewel caught his attention.

_____

Objective: to use punctuation to aid the reader

Name _____   Date _____

Verb tenses (past and present) (1)

Remember

We use the **past tense** to talk about the **past** e.g. Yesterday I **ate** an apple.
We use the **present tense** to talk about the **present** e.g. Now I **am eating** a pear.

- Play this game with a partner.
- Cut out the sentences and shuffle them up.
- Put them face down on the table.
- Take it in turns to turn over two sentences.
- If you turn over the same sentence in both the present and the past tense you keep them.
- If not, turn them face down again and continue the game.
- The winner is the person with most pairs of sentences at the end.

Present tense	Past tense
Emma is going to school.	Emma went to school.
Sam is digging the garden.	Sam dug the garden.
Joe is riding his bike.	Joe rode his bike.
The door is creaking.	The door creaked.
We are climbing a hill.	We climbed a hill.
The girls are feeding the dog.	The girls fed the dog.
I am buying some sweets.	I bought some sweets.
You are writing a letter.	You wrote a letter.
She is falling.	She fell.
The bird is flying in the sky.	The bird flew in the sky.
You are swimming in the sea.	You swam in the sea.
You are looking smart.	You looked smart.
They are sailing a boat.	They sailed a boat.

Objective: to revise work on past and present verb tenses

Verb tenses (past and present) (2)

We use the **past tense** to talk about the **past**
e.g. Yesterday I **ate** an apple.
We use the **present tense** to talk about the
present e.g. Now I **am eating** a pear.

Complete the table below.

verb	present tense	past tense
to crawl	I am crawling	I crawled
to come	I am coming	
to hop		
to drive		
to cry		
to hug		
to give		
to take		
to steal		
to eat		
to speak		
to wear		
to sing		
to freeze		
to forget		
to mix		

Objective: to revise work on past and present verb tenses

Verb tenses (past and present) (3)

Underline the verb in each sentence.
Rewrite the sentences.
Change each verb into the past tense.
The first is done for you.

1 The church clock <u>is striking</u> midnight.
  The church clock <u>struck</u> midnight.

2 The children are drawing a picture.
  _____

3 The girl is fighting with her brother.
  _____

4 The children are carrying their bags.
  _____

5 We are having a picnic in the park.
  _____

6 The dog is gnawing a bone.
  _____

7 The lady is pegging some washing on the line.
  _____

8 The man is shaking his fist.
  _____

9 The beanstalk is growing taller every day.
  _____

10 The boy is shutting the door.
  _____

Objective: to revise work on past and present verb tenses

Verb tenses (past, present and future) (1)

Remember

We use the **past tense** to talk about the **past** e.g.
Yesterday I **ate** an apple.
We use the **present tense** to talk about the **present** e.g.
Now I **am eating** a pear. We use the **future tense** to talk
about the **future** e.g. Next I **will eat** a peach.

Cut out these sentences. Sort them into three sets – sentences in the:
1) past tense   **2**) present tense   **3**) future tense

I am acting in a play.	Yesterday it snowed.
Will you call for me?	You are feeling happy.
At Christmas the girl got a bike.	Liverpool will win the game next week.
The boy is climbing a ladder.	I baked a cake on Sunday.
He will be ten next March.	A girl is skipping.
We went for a picnic.	I will go out after tea.
It is raining.	You got two sums wrong.
In the Summer we will go on holiday.	We are at school.
At midnight the aliens landed.	Sam will go to bed early tonight.
The children are sitting quietly.	Last week the boy fell over.
It will be sunny tomorrow.	We are playing in the park.

Objective: to revise work on past, present and future verb tenses

Verb tenses (past, present and future) (2)

We use the **past tense** to talk about the **past** e.g.
Yesterday I **ate** an apple.
We use the **present tense** to talk about the **present** e.g.
Now I **am eating** a pear. We use the **future tense** to talk
about the **future** e.g. Next I **will eat** a peach.

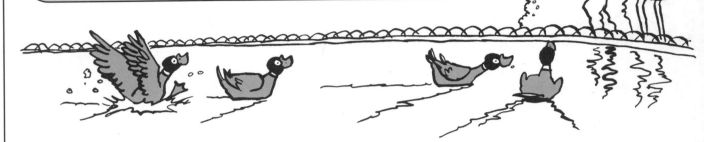

Underline the verbs in this story. They all in the past tense.

I got up late on Saturday. I went downstairs and ate my lunch. I watched cartoons
on TV for a while. Then I telephoned my friend. At two o'clock I rode my bike
round to my friend's house. We went to the park. We fed the ducks with some
bread. Then we bought some sweets. After this we played on the swings. At four
o'clock we returned to my house and had some tea. We played some games on my
computer. My friend went home at eight o'clock. I had a bath and then read a book
in bed.

Rewrite the story in the future tense. The first sentence is done for you. Continue on
the other side of the sheet if necessary

I will get up late on Sunday.

Objective: to revise work on past, present and future verb tenses

Verb tenses (past, present and future) (3)

Remember

We use the **past tense** to talk about the **past** e.g.
Yesterday I **ate** an apple.
We use the **present tense** to talk about the **present** e.g.
Now I **am eating** a pear. We use the **future tense** to talk
about the **future** e.g. Next I **will eat** a peach.

Underline the verb in each sentence.
The verbs are all in the present tense.
Rewrite each sentence in the past and future tense.
The first sentence is done for you.

1. The bells <u>are ringing</u> loudly.

   The bells rang loudly. (past)

   The bells will ring loudly. (future)

2. Mr Jones is growing some tomatoes.

   _____

   _____

3. Ben is tidying his bedroom.

   _____

   _____

4. We are swimming in the sea.

   _____

   _____

5. I am writing to my aunt.

   _____

   _____

6. You are feeling frightened.

   _____

   _____

Objective: to revise work on past, present and future verb tenses

Auxiliary verbs (1)

Sometimes we use an **auxiliary** (or **helper**) verb with the main verb. The auxiliary verb may give us **more information** about the **tense** of the verb e.g. I **am** eating (present tense), I **have** eaten (past tense) I **will** eat (future tense).

Underline the auxiliary verb in each sentence.
Say if the sentence is written in the past, present or future tense.
The first is done for you.

(1) William <u>is</u> watching television. (**present tense**)

(2) My mother was washing some clothes. (_____)

(3) I am doing some grammar exercises. (_____)

(4) The children were arguing loudly. (_____)

(5) I will call for you in the morning. (_____)

(6) I have visited the Tower of London. (_____)

(7) Sally has fallen in the mud. (_____)

(8) I will change into my best clothes for the party. (_____)

(9) My dog is sleeping in his basket. (_____)

(10) The cat was chasing some birds in the garden. (_____)

Objective: to investigate the use of auxiliary verbs

Auxiliary verbs (2)

Sometimes we use an **auxiliary** (or **helper**) verb with the main verb. The auxiliary verb may give us **more information** about the **tense** of the verb e.g. I **am** eating (present tense), I **have** eaten (past tense) I **will** eat (future tense).

Rewrite each sentence. Choose the best auxiliary verb to complete it.

(1) You (can/does) see the stars on a clear night.

_____

(2) I (am/are) going home soon.

_____

(3) John (is/are) waiting for his friend.

_____

(4) Mr Smith (has/have) been in France for a month.

_____

(5) What (was/did) your mother say when you were late?

_____

(6) (Shall/Do) you think football is silly?

_____

(7) The racing cars (were/can) travelling too fast round the corner.

_____

(8) Why (could/does) it always rain so much?

_____

(9) You (will/was) get wet if it rains.

_____

(10) The Queen (has/is) visited Edinburgh.

_____

Objective: to investigate the use of auxiliary verbs

Auxiliary verbs (3)

Sometimes we use an **auxiliary** (or **helper**) verb with the main verb. The auxiliary verb may give us **more information** about the **tense** of the verb e.g. I **am** eating (present tense), I **have** eaten (past tense) I **will** eat (future tense).

An auxiliary verb has been missed out of each sentence. Rewrite each sentence and think of a suitable auxiliary verb to complete it.

(1) Yesterday I feeling rather ill.

_____

(2) Next week I having a party.

_____

(3) My mum thought she won the lottery.

_____

(4) How long it take to learn to play a recorder?

_____

(5) "You help me?" the man asked the lady.

_____

(6) You not cross a busy road without looking.

_____

(7) Julia tried hard but she not keep a secret.

_____

(8) What you like to do at the weekend?

_____

(9) I give you a sweet if you let me play on your computer.

_____

(10) My dog eaten all his dinner.

_____

Verb forms (1)

Active verbs in these sentences have got muddled up.
Work out what the verbs should be.
Rewrite each sentence correctly.

(1) The man <u>gud</u> his garden.

_____

(2) The boy <u>erod</u> his bike.

_____

(3) The footballer <u>dikkec</u> the ball.

_____

(4) The choir <u>gans</u> a lovely song.

_____

(5) A rabbit <u>tea</u> a carrot.

_____

(6) The car <u>sdenarc</u> into the wall.

_____

(7) I <u>krand</u> the cold milk.

_____

(8) We <u>smaw</u> in the pool.

_____

(9) The girl <u>arn</u> all the way home.

_____

(10) A squirrel <u>bedmilc</u> the tree.

_____

Objective: to focus on different verb forms

Verb forms (2)

We use **different verb forms** in **different situations**.
We use the **interrogative** form of the verb when we
ask questions e.g. *Did* you *find* your shorts?

Match each statement with its interrogative form.
Underline the interrogative form of the verbs used.

Statement	Interrogative form
(1) The child crossed the road.	Was the dinner cooked?
(2) The car started first time.	Is Anna at the door?
(3) The dinner was cooked.	Did the child cross the road?
(4) James collects stamps.	Have you seen that film?
(5) She is called Amy.	Will we be on time?
(6) Anna is at the door.	Did the car start first time?
(7) We will be on time.	Does Mr Jones collect stamps?
(8) I have seen that film.	Is she called Amy?
(9) A lorry can go fast.	Do Arsenal play at Highbury?
(10) Arsenal play at Highbury.	Can a lorry go fast?

Objective: to focus on different verb forms

Verb forms (3)

Think of a suitable imperative verb to complete each gap.
Make your own nonsense rhyme using imperative verbs.

_____ a drum.	_____ your thumb.
_____ on the light.	_____ a fight.
_____ that thief!	_____ your teeth.
_____ to bed.	_____ on your head.
_____ a book.	_____ a look.
_____ the door.	_____ the floor.
_____ your tea.	_____ a tree.
_____ on that chair.	_____ your hair.
_____ in the bath.	_____ me laugh.
_____ the grass.	_____ out of a glass.
_____ the road.	_____ a toad.
_____ on your coat.	_____ the boat.
_____ a case.	_____ your face.
_____ your hand.	_____ to the band.
_____ a fish.	_____ a wish.

Objective: to focus on different verb forms

Name _____   Date _____

Verbs – 1st, 2nd and 3rd person (1)

Say in which person the
underlined pronouns are written.

1 <u>I</u> am reading a book.   (1st person singular)

2 <u>He</u> is riding a bike.   (_____)

3 <u>They</u> are on a train.   (_____)

4 "What are <u>you</u> doing?" the teacher asked Ben.   (_____)

5 <u>She</u> is packing her suitcase.   (_____)

6 <u>It</u> is going too fast.   (_____)

7 <u>We</u> are on our way home.   (_____)

8 "Where are <u>you</u> going?" the man asked the boys. (_____)

9 "May <u>I</u> come?" the girl asked.   (_____)

10 The men sat down when <u>they</u> had a break.   (_____)

11 "<u>You</u> can all do it," the teacher told the children. (_____)

12 When the squirrel came down <u>it</u> hopped on the grass. (_____)

Objective: to investigate the use of the 1st, 2nd and 3rd person

Verbs – 1st, 2nd and 3rd person (2)

A piece of writing may be written in:
the **1st person** when it is about **ourselves**
e.g. **I** (singular), **we** (plural)
the **2nd person** when it is about **you**
e.g. **you** (may be singular or plural)
the **3rd person** when it is about **others**
e.g. **he**, **she**, **it** (singular), **they** (plural).

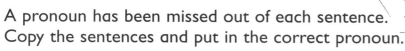

A pronoun has been missed out of each sentence.
Copy the sentences and put in the correct pronoun.

1 began to rain hard. (3rd person singular)

_____

2 Will shut the door, please? (2nd person singular)

_____

3 love eating fruit. (1st person singular)

_____

4 played hide and seek in the park. (3rd person plural)

_____

5 Emma is a kind girl. loves to help everyone. (3rd person singular)

_____

6 Ben picked up his bag. looked inside it. (3rd person singular)

_____

7 "know how to get there," the children shouted to their dad. (1st person plural)

_____

8 "Stop shouting, children. are giving me a headache!" the teacher said. (2nd person plural)

_____

9 When the robot entered stared at me. (3rd person singular)

_____

10 "Can come?" the children shouted excitely. (1st person plural)

_____

Verbs – 1st, 2nd and 3rd person (3)

A piece of writing may be written in:
the **1st person** when it is about **ourselves**
e.g. **I** (singular), **we** (plural)
the **2nd person** when it is about **you**
e.g. **you** (may be singular or plural)
the **3rd person** when it is about **others**
e.g. **he**, **she**, **it** (singular), **they** (plural).

(1) This story is written in the 3rd person. Underline all the pronouns in it.

> Tom did not like walking home across the dark common at night. He began to imagine all sorts of things. He thought he could hear strange sounds all around. Tom decided to run. Just then he was sure he heard a very strange humming noise. He stopped. He peered into the darkness. There, in the distance, he could see an eerie light glowing in the sky. Tom stared in amazement as a weird space craft landed in front of his very eyes. He watched in horror as the door opened.

(2) Now write the story in the 1st person as if you were Tom.
The first sentence is done for you.

> I did not like walking home across the dark common at night.

(3) Continue the story on the other side of this sheet in your own words.

Objective: to investigate the use of the 1st, 2nd and 3rd person

Common and proper nouns (1)

Remember

A **common noun** is a **general name** of a **person** (e.g. a teacher), a **place** (e.g. a library) or a **thing** (e.g. a car).

Cut out these common nouns.
Sort them into three sets:
Set 1) names of people
Set 2) names of places
Set 3) names of things
There are eight nouns in each set.

teacher	harbour	apple	dentist
garage	hangar	bike	greengrocer
bottle	bank	artist	library
pen	church	window	stadium
musician	brick	builder	computer
factory	author	book	sailor

Objective: to revise common and proper nouns

Common and proper nouns (2)

Remember

A **common noun** is a **general name** of a **person** (e.g. a teacher), a **place** (e.g. a library) or a **thing** (e.g. a car). A **proper noun** is the **particular name** of a **person** (e.g. Mrs Jones), a **place** (e.g. Luton) or a **thing** (e.g. Tower Bridge). N.B. Proper nouns always begin with **capital letters**.

1 Write each noun in the correct column of the chart below.

The Pyramids	April	Mrs Barnes	rabbit
table	River Thames	telephone	Dublin
The Planetarium	hill	Spain	Easter
ruler	paper	Saturday	India
star	Venus	Dr Luke	Vauxhall
Daily Mirror	nurse	New York	ant
tree	Beech Road	The Twits	king

common nouns	proper nouns

2 Add four more nouns to each set.

Objective: to revise common and proper nouns

Common and proper nouns (3)

Rewrite these sentences.
Punctuate them correctly.
Underline the common nouns.

(1) ben nevis is the highest mountain in britain

_____

(2) dundee is a big city in scotland

_____

(3) do you read the newspaper called the daily mail

_____

(4) my birthday is in september

_____

(5) christopher columbus was a famous explorer

_____

(6) we are staying in a hotel in canterbury it is called the grand

_____

(7) the plane from bombay landed at heathrow airport in london

_____

(8) my favourite author is roald dahl

_____

(9) we sailed down the river thames in a boat

_____

(10) i like television i always watch coronation street

_____

Objective: to revise common and proper nouns

Concrete and abstract nouns (1)

Concrete nouns are the names of things you can **touch**, **taste**, **see**, **hear** or **smell** e.g. car. **Abstract nouns** are names of **thoughts**, **ideas** and **feelings**. You **cannot** touch, taste, see, hear or smell them e.g. strength.

Write each noun in the correct column of the chart below.

bread	honesty	car	pencil	loneliness	wonder
door	horror	beauty	dog	nastiness	cup
advice	book	grass	relief	wheel	thought
ant	leaf	tiredness	roof	flight	action

concrete nouns	abstract nouns

Concrete and abstract nouns (2)

Concrete nouns are the names of things you can **touch**, **taste**, **see**, **hear** or **smell** e.g. car. **Abstract nouns** are names of **thoughts**, **ideas** and **feelings**. You **cannot** touch, taste, see, hear or smell them e.g. strength.

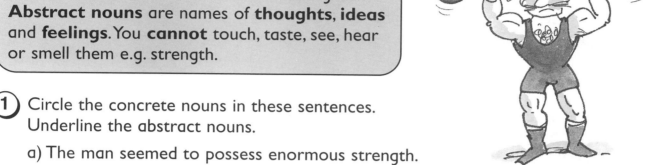

① Circle the concrete nouns in these sentences. Underline the abstract nouns.

a) The man seemed to possess enormous strength.

b) The small girl showed great courage when she faced the big bully.

c) There was a look of love in the mother's eyes as she held her baby.

d) The astronaut stared in fear at the alien.

e) The thief caused misery to many people.

f) The child had a belief that one day he would become a famous inventor.

g) The judge praised the witness for her honesty.

h) There is always danger when you climb high mountains.

② Make up some sentences of your own. Use these abstract nouns in them:

| joy | foolishness | height | patience | astonishment | poverty |

a) _____

b) _____

c) _____

d) _____

e) _____

f) _____

Concrete and abstract nouns (3)

⭐ **Remember**

Concrete nouns are the names of things you can **touch**, **taste**, **see**, **hear** or **smell** e.g. car.
Abstract nouns are names of **thoughts**, **ideas** and **feelings**. You **cannot** touch, taste, see, hear or smell them e.g. strength.

1 Write the adjective from which each of these abstract nouns comes. The first is done for you.

a) loyalty – loyal

b) sickness – _____

c) ugliness – _____

d) height – _____

e) width – _____

f) heat – _____

g) darkness – _____

h) foolishness – _____

i) clarity – _____

j) wealthy – _____

2 Change each of these verbs into abstract nouns by adding a suffix. The first is done for you.

a) accept – acceptance

b) attract – _____

c) hate – _____

d) please – _____

e) judge – _____

f) satisfy – _____

g) fly – _____

h) divide – _____

i) obey – _____

j) astonish – _____

k) rely – _____

l) clean – _____

m) concentrate – _____

n) persuade – _____

Objective: to explore concrete and abstract nouns

Pronouns (1)

Remember

A **pronoun** is a word that **takes the place of a noun**
e.g. Anna ate **her** (Anna's) tea when **she** (Anna) got home.

Copy the sentences.
Choose the best pronoun for each sentence.

(1) The cat ate the food because (you/it) was hungry.

_____

(2) The girl smiled when (he/she) saw her friend.

_____

(3) (I/She) love listening to music.

_____

(4) When the police arrived, (we/they) arrested the burglar.

_____

(5) "Can you help (you/us)?" Sam and Ben asked Tom.

_____

(6) When the queen came in, (he/she) stumbled and fell.

_____

(7) Are (it/you) going out tonight?

_____

(8) (They/It) is very rainy and wet today.

_____

(9) The man spoke to the lady and asked (him/her) the way to the shops.

_____

(10) I like Jamie but (we/he) does not like (us/me).

_____

Objective: to revise some of the functions of pronouns

Pronouns (2)

Remember

A **pronoun** is a word that **takes the place of a noun** e.g. Anna ate **her** (Anna's) tea when **she** (Anna) got home.

Write who or what each underlined pronoun stands for.

(1) The man picked up the case and carried <u>it</u> (_____) into the hotel.

(2) Sarah has a dog. <u>She</u> (_____) takes <u>it</u> (_____) for long walks.

(3) "<u>I</u> (_____) support Chelsea," Liam said.

(4) "Let <u>us</u> (_____) come with <u>you</u> (_____)," Mark and John said to Cara.

(5) The man tried to drive the lorry but <u>it</u> (_____) was too hard

for <u>him</u> (_____).

(6) The children wanted to play with their friends but <u>they</u> (_____) out.

(7) "Are <u>you</u> (_____) ready?" Mrs Andrews asked Ben and Rosa.

(8) When Dan saw the baby, <u>he</u> (_____) spoke to <u>her</u> (_____).

(9) The boys tried hard but <u>they</u> (_____) could not beat the girls.

(10) "<u>We</u> (_____) like <u>it</u> (_____)," Mr and Mrs Smith said when <u>they</u>

(_____) saw the new house.

Objective: to revise some of the functions of pronouns

Pronouns (3)

Rewrite these sentences.
Replace some of the nouns with pronouns to make them sound less clumsy.

1 James hit out at the ball, but James missed the ball.

_____

2 Ben was watching the cartoon but the cartoon bored Ben.

_____

3 Shannon asked Shannon's mother if Shannon could have a drink.

_____

4 Mark said to Amy, "Would you pass Mark's pencil, please?"

_____

5 Ali asked his friends if Ali could play.

_____

6 The doctor told Mrs Saunders that the doctor would call on Mrs Saunders as soon as possible.

_____

_____

7 The children sulked angrily when the children were told off.

_____

8 The pilot said that the pilot had to make an emergency landing.

_____

9 The queen told the king that the queen wanted the king to buy the queen a diamond necklace for the queen's birthday.

_____

_____

10 Sam and Tom said, "Do you like Sam and Tom's picture?"

_____

Objective: to revise some of the functions of pronouns

Homonyms (1)

Match up the pairs of sentences which contain the same homonym.
Underline the homonym in both sentences which is the same.

I went out with my <u>mummy</u>.	My chest ached.
The light was too bright.	I cannot lift heavy weights.
I opened the old chest.	They saw a <u>mummy</u> in the museum.
The water tank was empty.	I went to lie on my bed.
The lift got stuck between floors.	The case was quite light.
The old man had a walking stick.	My dog has a loud bark.
You should never lie.	The army tank was noisy.
The train leaves at six o'clock.	I swam to the river bank.
The bark of the tree was rough.	The trees lost their leaves.
I put my money in the bank.	You stick stamps on envelopes.

Objective: to explore homonyms and ambiguity

Homonyms (2)

Remember

A **homonym** is a word which may have the **same spelling as another** but has a **different meaning** e.g. a *wave* of the hand; a *wave* at sea. This can sometimes lead to confusion. The meaning may be **ambiguous** (unclear).

Write examples of the words in both columns.

homonym	when used as a noun	when used as a verb
bear	a type of animal	to <u>bear</u> pain
watch		
break		
roar		
row		
waste		
wind		
check		
coach		
stamp		

Objective: to explore homonyms and ambiguity

Homonyms (3)

Remember

A **homonym** is a word which may have the **same spelling as another** but has a **different meaning** e.g. a *wave* of the hand; a *wave* at sea. This can sometimes lead to confusion. The meaning may be **ambiguous** (unclear).

wave

wave

Make up pairs of sentences using the homonyms below.
Make sure that the same homonym must have a different meaning in each of your sentences. Continue on the other side of the sheet.

| ring | dress | spring | race | swallow |
| palm | patient | trunk | fire | play |

1 _____

_____

2 _____

_____

3 _____

_____

4 _____

_____

5 _____

_____

6 _____

_____

7 _____

_____

Objective: to explore homonyms and ambiguity

Ambiguity (1)

Remember

Sometimes when we write things we do not make the meaning clear enough. The meaning is **ambiguous** e.g. I like to eat myself = I like eating.

Choose the best meaning for each underlined word from the glossary at the bottom of the page.

Meaning of the underlined word

1) I ate a <u>date</u>.

a type of fruit _____

2) Queen Elizabeth is our <u>ruler</u>.

_____

3) The <u>swallow</u> laid its eggs.

_____

4) The <u>bank</u> was shut.

_____

5) Keep a <u>watch</u> out.

_____

6) The <u>sink</u> was blocked.

_____

7) He gave me a <u>tap</u> on the back.

_____

8) I put a <u>letter</u> in the post-box.

_____

GLOSSARY

bank	a) where money is kept	b) the side of a river
date	a) a type of fruit	b) a particular time
letter	a) we use these to make words	b) an envelope
ruler	a) you measure with it	b) a king or queen
sink	a) something for holding water	b) the opposite of float
swallow	a) a bird	b) what you do when you drink
tap	a) a gentle blow	b) where water comes from
watch	a) observe carefully	b) a time-piece

Objective: to explore ambiguity

Ambiguity (2)

☆ **Remember**

Sometimes when we write things we do not make the meaning clear enough. The meaning is **ambiguous** e.g. I like to eat myself = I like eating.

Cut out the sentences. Match each ambiguous sentence with the sentence which makes its meaning clear.

Ambiguous sentences

I feel like a hamburger.

Car for sale. Suitable for young person with sunroof.

Lost. Dog belonging to Fred Smith with long black hair.

Did you see the programme about sunbathing on TV?

Girl hits boy with can of drink.

I visited my aunt in London where she lives on Sunday.

The police stopped a truck with a cow that had a puncture.

Reporter talks to mother of ten.

Unambiguous sentences

On Sunday I visited my aunt who lives in London.

Lost. Dog with a long black hair. Belongs to Fred Smith.

The police stopped a truck that had a puncture. There was a cow on the truck.

I would like a hamburger to eat.

A reporter interviews a mother who has ten children.

Did you see the programme on television about sunbathing?

Car with a sunroof for sale. Suitable for a young person.

A girl hit a boy. The boy had a can of drink.

Objective: to explore ambiguity

Ambiguity (3)

Remember

Sometimes when we write things we do not make the meaning clear enough. The meaning is **ambiguous** e.g. I like to eat myself = I like eating.

Rewrite each sentence to make its meaning clearer.
Use the clues in the brackets to help you.

(1)

Wanted
Bath for baby
with tin bottom

(Who or what has a tin bottom?)

_____

(2) There is a cherry tree in the garden that needs attention.
(What needs attention – the garden or the cherry tree?)

_____

(3) Jumping on the bus, the conductor asked me for my fare.
(Who jumped on the bus?)

_____

(4) Only proper shoes are to be worn to school. (Is that all? Nothing else?!)

_____

(5) I took out my muddy shirt from my bag and threw it into the washing machine.
(What was thrown into the washing machine – the bag or the shirt?)

_____

(6) Tom enjoyed chips more than his friends. (Didn't Tom like his friends?)

_____

(7) Angry footballer shouts at referee with whistle. (Can whistles shout?)

_____

(8) Children make a wonderful snack. (Are children good to eat?)

_____

Objective: to explore ambiguity

Summarising (1)

Remember

Summarising means **shortening** a text **without losing its meaning**. Sometimes we use **abbreviations** to shorten words and phrases e.g. PTO = please turn over.

- Play this game with a partner.
- Cut out the abbreviations and their meanings.
- Place them face down on the table.
- Take it in turns to turn over two 'cards'.
- If you turn over an abbreviation and its meaning you keep them.
- If not, turn the 'cards' face down again and continue the game.
- The winner is the person with most abbreviations and correct meanings at the end.

Abbreviations

Mr	Rd	St	Ave
Sq	Rev	kph	NB
etc	BC	PS	GB
USA	RSVP	PTO	Dr
cm	BBC	kg	via

Meanings

Reverend	et cetera (and so on)	British Broadcasting Corporation	United States of America
Road	Avenue	Nota Bene (note well)	by way of
please turn over	Square	doctor	répondez s'il vous plaît (please reply)
Great Britain	post scriptum	kilometres per hour	kilogram
Mister	Street	before Christ	centimetre

Objective: to construct texts in different ways without losing their meaning

Summarising (2)

Summarising means **shortening** a text **without losing its meaning**. Sometimes one word may be used for several, as in **definitions** e.g. arrive = to come to the end of a journey.

Write one word for each definition. Each word begins with 'b'.

1 _ _ _ _ _ _ a kind of flag

2 _ _ _ _ _ _ _ a platform with a rail round it, outside an upstairs window

3 _ _ _ _ a very young child

4 _ _ _ an animal like a mouse with wings

5 _ _ _ _ _ _ to shout and make a lot of noise like an angry bull

6 _ _ _ _ _ _ _ a thick cover used on a bed

7 _ _ _ _ _ _ a hat tied under the chin or part of a car covering the engine

8 _ _ _ _ _ _ a piece of jewellery worn pinned to clothing

9 _ _ _ _ _ to open and close your eyes quickly

10 _ _ _ _ _ _ _ _ a house without any upstairs rooms

Objective: to construct texts in different ways without losing their meaning

Summarising (3)

Underline the most important words in each sentence.
Then write each paragraph of information in note-form.

What pandas look like
The panda has a fat body, a round face, small ears and a black patch around each eye. It has a furry black and white coat which is very thick. Its coat keeps the panda warm in cold weather. The panda's coat is also waterproof and keeps out the rain.

What pandas eat
A panda has big strong teeth and jaws. It eats huge amounts of bamboo. This is a kind of woody plant and is very tough. Pandas spend about fourteen hours each day eating and the rest of the time they spend asleep.

Baby pandas
Baby pandas are called cubs. They are tiny when they are born. The mother panda looks after her cubs until they are old enough to live alone. This is when they are about eighteen months old. Pandas are now only found in China.

Using fewer words (1)

Remember

We can sometimes **shorten** sentences by using **fewer words** e.g. 'Ben is not very well.' may be written as 'Ben is ill.'

Rewrite each sentence.
Choose the best word to replace the underlined phrases.

| speechless | carefully | gently | fashionably | dangerous |
| silently | difficult | suddenly | thirsty | soon |

1 Swimming in the river was <u>full of danger</u>.

_____

2 The nurse bandaged my arm <u>with great care</u>.

_____

3 The duchess always dressed <u>in the latest fashions</u>.

_____

4 The cat crept up on the birds <u>without any noise</u>.

_____

5 Climbing the steep mountain was <u>not very easy</u>.

_____

6 <u>All at once</u> it began to rain.

_____

7 <u>In a short time</u> the ambulance arrived.

_____

8 The dog was <u>in need of a drink</u>.

_____

9 Emma stroked the cat <u>in a gentle manner</u>.

_____

10 Tom was so surprised at winning he was <u>unable to speak</u>.

_____

Objective: to construct sentences in different ways, whilst retaining their meaning

Using fewer words (2)

Remember

We can sometimes **shorten** sentences by using **fewer words** e.g. 'The ~~hot~~ sun shone ~~brightly~~ in the sky.' may be written as 'The sun shone in the sky.'

Underline the adjectives and adverbs in these sentences.
Rewrite each sentence, leaving out all the adjectives and adverbs.

1 The angry motorist shouted loudly at the foolish pedestrian.

_____

2 The handsome jockey jumped quickly onto the white horse.

_____

3 Suddenly the speeding car raced past noisily.

_____

4 The old lady trudged slowly up the steep hill.

_____

5 Some huge black clouds gathered menacingly in the sky.

_____

6 The glamorous actress stepped boldly towards the cameras.

_____

7 Miserably the soaking runner crossed the finishing line.

_____

8 The enormous waves crashed continuously on the rocks.

_____

9 The hungry man ordered a big meal and ate it ravenously.

_____

10 Bravely the courageous knight faced the fierce dragon.

_____

Objective: to construct sentences in different ways, whilst retaining their meaning

Using fewer words (3)

Remember

We can sometimes **shorten** sentences by using **fewer words** e.g. 'I saw the man. He stroked the dog.' may be written as 'I saw the man stroking the dog.'

Think of a way of rewriting each pair of sentences as one sentence, using fewer words, without changing the meaning.

(1) My friend stood at the door. He was holding a present for me.

_____

(2) The girl was thirsty. She asked for a drink.

_____

(3) I went to bed. I felt very tired.

_____

(4) The car was old and rusty. It was outside our house.

_____

(5) The small child stood up. She clapped her hands with happiness.

_____

(6) The rain was heavy. It flooded the street.

_____

(7) I stood for a while. I watched the procession pass by.

_____

(8) Tom's bag was heavy. It was full of apples, pears and bananas.

_____

(9) I woke up. I wondered what to do.

_____

(10) My dad washed up the dishes. They were very greasy.

_____

Objective: to construct sentences in different ways, whilst retaining their meaning

Experimenting with words (1)

Remember

Sometimes we can **substitute words** in sentences **without changing the meaning** e.g.
The tiny (small) baby was crying.

Rewrite each sentence. Replace the underlined word.
Make the new sentence mean the same.
Choose the best word to help you.

1 I heard a loud <u>moaning</u> noise. (heavy, groaning)

_____

2 The house was very <u>new</u>. (modern, brave)

_____

3 The elephant <u>walked</u> through the forest. (ran, lumbered)

_____

4 When I saw the monster it gave me a <u>fright</u>. (scare, light)

_____

5 I thought it was a <u>mad</u> idea. (crazy, good)

_____

6 The woman was very <u>slender</u>. (dry, slim)

_____

7 I looked at my present in <u>surprise</u>. (astonishment, danger)

_____

8 The men <u>commenced</u> work at eight o'clock. (finished, started)

_____

9 The clock struck <u>midday</u>. (midnight, noon)

_____

10 After the game, the player felt very <u>weary</u>. (happy, tired)

_____

Objective: to discover how substituting words may affect the meaning of sentences

Experimenting with words (2)

Remember

Sometimes we can **substitute words** in sentences **without changing the meaning** e.g. The tiny (small) baby was crying.

Rewrite each sentence.
Think of a five-letter word to replace the underlined word.
Do not change the meaning of the sentence.

1 Two clowns <u>attempted</u> to make the crowd laugh.

_____

2 The captain refused to <u>abandon</u> the sinking ship.

_____

3 The soldier was given a medal for <u>courageous</u> behaviour.

_____

4 The flower bed is <u>circular</u>.

_____

5 I like a nice cold <u>beverage</u> when I am hot and thirsty.

_____

6 It was <u>fortunate</u> there wasn't a bad accident.

_____

7 There was a bad <u>smell</u> coming from the dustbin.

_____

8 It was obvious that the man was <u>intoxicated.</u>

_____

9 Our teacher gave us a <u>brief</u> break after the test.

_____

10 We asked if there were any <u>vacant</u> rooms at the hotel.

_____

Objective: to discover how substituting words may affect the meaning of sentences

Experimenting with words (3)

Remember

Sometimes we can **substitute words** in sentences **without changing the meaning** e.g.
The tiny (small) baby was crying.
Sometimes substituting words **changes the meaning** e.g.
It was a difficult (simple) task.

Rewrite each sentence.
Replace the underlined word.
Make the new sentence mean the opposite.

1 Huge crowds cheered the pop group on their <u>arrival</u>.

_____

2 Uncle Sam <u>often</u> comes to see me.

_____

3 My writing seems to be getting <u>better</u>.

_____

4 The blade of the knife is very <u>sharp</u>.

_____

5 The prisoner was found <u>guilty</u>.

_____

6 The guests arrived <u>late</u> that morning.

_____

7 The strange liquid turned out to be quite <u>harmful</u>.

_____

8 The water in the well is <u>impure</u>.

_____

9 The teacher spoke to the <u>rude</u> child.

_____

10 The lady was full of <u>hatred</u>.

_____

Objective: to discover how substituting words may affect the meaning of sentences

Prepositions (1)

Remember

A **preposition** is a word that shows the **relationship** of one thing to another. Prepositions often tell us about **position** e.g. The apple was **in** the bag.

Write them here.

1) Find ten prepositions hidden in this puzzle.

q	w	u	p	x	a	r	d	r	e
t	y	p	z	d	o	w	n	a	s
a	o	f	f	d	f	g	h	j	k
l	m	n	b	v	x	o	v	e	r
z	v	u	n	d	e	r	h	g	t
w	t	q	r	o	u	n	d	f	g
h	b	v	b	e	t	w	e	e	n
u	p	o	n	b	h	y	r	w	d
q	w	a	b	o	v	e	k	l	j
m	n	v	b	e	l	o	w	x	z

up

_____

_____

_____

_____

_____

_____

_____

_____

2) Draw

a book
under the table

a bird
above the tree

a circle
inside the square

a bike
outside the shop

Objective: to understand the function of prepositions

Prepositions (2)

Rewrite each sentence.
Think of a suitable preposition to go where one is missing.

1 The child hid∧the bed.

_____

2 You get∧of a car.

_____

3 The horse galloped∧the field.

_____

4 You dive∧a swimming pool.

_____

5 The child stood∧his parents.

_____

6 You climb∧a mountain.

_____

7 The plane flew∧the town.

_____

8 You cross∧a bridge.

_____

9 A train goes∧a tunnel.

_____

10 You jump∧a narrow stream.

_____

Objective: to understand the function of prepositions

Prepositions (3)

Remember

A **preposition** is a word that shows the **relationship** of one thing to another. Prepositions often tell us about **position** e.g. The apple was **in** the bag.

① Think of a suitable preposition to complete each of the following phrases:

to protest _____	to be guilty _____
to be angry _____	to be inspired _____
to rely _____	to be different _____
to shrink _____	to be satisfied _____
to be the opposite _____	to be a victim _____

② Make up some sentences of your own and use all the phrases you made above in them.

a) _____

b) _____

c) _____

d) _____

e) _____

f) _____

g) _____

h) _____

i) _____

j) _____

Objective: to understand the function of prepositions

Name _____ Date _____

Speaking and writing (1)

Cut out the sentences.
Sort them into two sets:
– sentences in Standard English
– sentences in non-standard English.
There will be ten in each set.

Pass me my book, please.	You comin wiv me or what?
I ain't going out.	Let me have a look.
Get lost, will ya?	I'm not going there again.
I can't stand that kid.	There were lots of crisps in the bag.
I have given my toys away.	You must of got a lot of sweets.
My friend and I went to the shops.	I saw my friend at school.
I'm going home soon.	Give us me ball back.
We seen 'im yesterday.	I found my book what I'd lost.
You'll never win nothing.	I got all my spellings wrong.
I was very hungry.	Someone's pinched me pencil.

Objective: to explore some of the differences between spoken and written English

Speaking and writing (2)

Remember

When we **speak**, we often use **non-standard English**
e.g. Where you goin'?
When we **write** we should use **Standard English**
e.g. Where are you going?

Some people in London use Cockney rhyming slang when speaking.
For example – 'apples and pears' means 'stairs.'
Cut out the phrases and their meanings.
Match them up.

Cockney rhyming slang

bacon and eggs	bees and honey	boat race
cat and mouse	daisy roots	dog and bone
frog and toad	Hampstead Heath	jam jar
loaf of bread	Lucy Locket	mince pies
Mother Hubbard	north and south	plates of meat
rabbit and pork	tea leaf	trouble and strife
whistle and flute	dickory dock	Barnet Fair

Meanings

thief	clock	head	house	mouth	legs	road
feet	suit	pocket	boots	talk	teeth	eyes
money	hair	face	phone	cupboard	wife	car

Objective: to explore some of the differences between spoken and written English

Speaking and writing (3)

When we **speak**, we often use
Non-standard English
e.g. Where you goin'?
When we **write** we should use
Standard English
e.g. Where are you going?

Write down what you think each of these non-standard English sentences means.

1) You've gorra be kidding!

2) Me and Tom went to town.

3) She woz real mad.

4) I ripped me shorts.

5) I'm gonna get yer!

6) What you done that for?

7) We 'ad to git out quick.

8) We wasn't doing nuffin' wrong.

9) I don't wanna go 'ome.

10) Me pencil was broke.

1) _____

2) _____

3) _____

4) _____

5) _____

6) _____

7) _____

8) _____

9) _____

10) _____

Objective: to explore some of the differences between spoken and written English

Apostrophes showing ownership (1)

We use an **apostrophe** to **show ownership** (to show that something belongs to someone). When the owner is **singular**, we usually write **'s** after the noun e.g. the **clown's** hat = the hat belonging to the clown.

Complete this chart:

short form with apostrophe	longer form
the clown's hat	the hat belonging to the clown
the girl's shoe	
the boy's cap	
the teacher's book	
the doctor's bag	
the horse's tail	
the bike's bell	
	the robe belonging to the king
	the card belonging to Tom
	the hat belonging to the lady
	the cow belonging to the farmer
	the case belonging to Mr Shah
	the egg belonging to the hen
	the trunk belonging to the elephant

Objective: to revise the use of apostrophes to show ownership

Apostrophes showing ownership (2)

Remember

We use an **apostrophe** to **show ownership**.

Rule 1 Many **plural** nouns end in **s**. To show ownership we put the apostrophe **after the s** e.g. the girls' bags = the bags belonging to the girls.

Rule 2 When a plural noun does **not** end with **s**, we show ownership by **adding 's** e.g. the men's car = the car belonging to the men.

Complete this chart:

short form with apostrophe	longer form
the ants' nest	the nest belonging to the ants
the teachers' car park	
the sailors' ship	
the cubs' camp	
the girls' toys	
the elephants' tusks	
	the book belonging to the children
	the tank belonging to the fish
	the ball belonging to the men
	the shop belonging to the women
	the wool belonging to the sheep
	the antlers belonging to the deer
	the feathers belonging to the geese

Objective: to revise the use of apostrophes to show ownership

Apostrophes showing ownership (3)

Remember

We use an **apostrophe** to **show ownership**.
Rule 1 When the owner is **singular**, we usually
write **'s** after the noun e.g. the **clown's** hat =
the hat belonging to the clown.
Rule 2 Many **plural** nouns end in **s**. To show
ownership we put the apostrophe **after the s**
e.g. the girls' bags = the bags belonging to the
girls.
Rule 3 When a plural noun does **not** end with **s**,
we show ownership by **adding 's** e.g. the men's
car = the car belonging to the men.

Explain the difference between each of these pairs of phrases.

1 a) the mouse's whiskers   b) the mice's whiskers

  The whiskers belonging to the mouse.   The whiskers belonging to the mice.

2 a) the potato's roots   b) the potatoes' roots

_____

3 a) the woman's bags   b) the women's bags

_____

4 a) the dog's dinner   b) the dogs' dinner

_____

5 a) the bird's eggs   b) the birds' eggs

_____

6 a) the child's toys   b) the children's toys

_____

7 a) the baby's rattle   b) the babies' rattle

_____

8 a) the horse's stable   b) the horses' stable

_____

9 a) the thief's hideout   b) the thieves' hideout

_____

10 a) the church's bells   b) the churches' bells

_____

Objective: to revise the use of apostrophes to show ownership

Clauses (1)

Remember

A **clause** is a **group of words** which may be used as a **whole sentence**, or as **part of a sentence**. A clause must contain a **subject** and a **verb** e.g. The prince lived in a castle. (This is a **one-clause** sentence.)

Underline the subject and circle the verb in each of these one-clause sentences.

(**1**) The pop singer (played) a guitar.

(**2**) The girl knocked on the door.

(**3**) The sheep were grazing in the field.

(**4**) A green monster appeared from behind the rock.

(**5**) Dan drank a large can of fizzy lemonade.

(**6**) Whales swim under the water most of the time.

(**7**) Our teacher drives a new car to school.

(**8**) We found an old chest in the cave.

(**9**) Foxes hunt at night-time.

(**10**) The huge giant stamped his foot angrily.

Objective: to investigate clauses

Clauses (2)

Remember

A **clause** is a **group of words** which may be used as a **whole sentence**, or as **part of a sentence**. A clause must contain a **subject** and a **verb** e.g. The prince lived in a castle. (This is a **one-clause** sentence.)

Choose the correct subject from the box to complete each of the one-clause sentences. Underline the verb in each sentence to make sure there is only one!

The surgeon	We	A helicopter	The referee	100 metres
Some snakes	The scientist	Mount Everest	Pandas	An astronaut

1 ☐ blew the whistle at the end of the football match.

2 ☐ invented a wonderful new washing machine.

3 ☐ eat bamboo shoots.

4 ☐ are poisonous.

5 ☐ is the highest mountain in the world.

6 ☐ make one kilometre.

7 ☐ rescued the sailors off the sinking ship.

8 ☐ operated on the patient.

9 ☐ get oil from under the ground.

10 ☐ flew the rocket.

Objective: to investigate clauses

Clauses (3)

Remember

A **clause** is a **group of words** which may be used as a **whole sentence**, or as **part of a sentence**. A clause must contain a **subject** and a **verb** e.g. The prince lived in a castle. (This is a **one-clause** sentence.)

The verb in each of these one-clause sentences is missing.
Think of a suitable verb and rewrite each sentence.
Underline the subject in each sentence.

(1) The owl for food in the wood.

_____

(2) The farmer his field with a tractor.

_____

(3) The stars brightly in the night sky.

_____

(4) Some birds nests in trees.

_____

(5) Many cars unleaded petrol.

_____

(6) A large jumbo jet on the runway.

_____

(7) Crowds of people the big match.

_____

(8) French people on the right-hand side of the road.

_____

(9) Tarantulas huge and hairy.

_____

(10) Deciduous trees their leaves in the autumn.

_____

Objective: to investigate clauses

More about clauses (1)

Remember

A **clause** is a **group of words** which may be used as a **whole sentence**, or as **part of a sentence**. A clause must contain a **subject** and a **verb** e.g. The pirate smiled (*clause 1*) as he opened the treasure chest (*clause 2*). (This is a **two-clause** sentence.)

Match up the beginning and ending of each two-clause sentence. Underline the verb in each clause and check that each sentence contains two verbs.

1 I did my homework   when he got lost.

2 My teacher was angry   as soon as we arrived there.

3 The child cried   when it skidded in some mud.

4 Everyone clapped   before I went to bed.

5 I fell off my bike   when the class made a lot of noise.

6 I went straight in the museum   as I received the prize.

7 I don't like apples   even though it was raining.

8 I went out to play   so I only eat bananas.

Objective: to investigate clauses further

More about clauses (2)

Cut out these sentences.
Underline the verbs in them.
Divide the sentences into two sets:
a) sentences containing one clause
b) sentences containing two clauses.
(There will be five sentences in each set.)

The hedgehog rolled up into a prickly ball.

I liked our holiday because we went to the seaside.

The moon came out and the stars twinkled.

I ate the burger and French fries hungrily.

The story ended in an exciting way.

Lions roar when they are angry.

I bought an ice cream when I got my pocket money.

The lady drove the silver sports car very fast.

The ship stayed in the harbour because the sea was too rough.

The wind blew the litter all over the place.

Objective: to investigate clauses further

More about clauses (3)

Remember

A **clause** is a **group of words** which may be used as a **whole sentence**, or as **part of a sentence**. A clause must contain a **subject** and a **verb** e.g. The pirate smiled (*clause 1*) as he opened the treasure chest (*clause 2*). (This is a **two-clause** sentence.)

Each of these sentences contains two clauses. Rewrite each sentence as two separate sentences containing one clause. Underline the verbs in the sentences you write. The first is done for you.

1 Emma shut the door but she opened the window.

Emma <u>shut</u> the door. She <u>opened</u> the window.

2 My dog is too fat because it eats too much.

_____

3 The sun came out so we went for a picnic.

_____

4 We went into the fast food restaurant and we ordered some burgers.

_____

5 I got all my spellings wrong but Amy scored top marks.

_____

6 I like swimming but I can't dive very well.

_____

7 The boy bought some sweets and ate them greedily.

_____

8 We left home after breakfast but we stopped after two hours for a break.

_____

9 The man bought some bricks with which he built a wall.

_____

10 I tried to solve the puzzle but it was too hard for me.

_____

Objective: to investigate clauses further

Connectives (1)

Choose the best connective to join these two clauses together.
Write the sentences you make.

1 The doctor examined the boy (which/who) had a broken leg.

_____

2 I will not speak to Amy (because/unless) I do not like her.

_____

3 It was foggy (since/so) it was difficult to see.

_____

4 I like to play outside (and/whenever) it snows.

_____

5 I watched the film (although/while) the acting was terrible.

_____

6 I saved all my pocket money (if/so that) I could buy the video game.

_____

7 I read a book (while/before) I went to sleep.

_____

8 I went to bed (whenever/after) the sun went down.

_____

9 I waited for my friend (because/until) he had finished his work.

_____

10 I will go (as long as/therefore) you come with me.

_____

Objective: to use connectives to join clauses together

Connectives (2)

Circle the connectives and underline the clauses they join in these sentences. The first is done for you.

1 I can jump on my bed (as often as) I like.

2 You cannot have any pocket money unless you tidy your room.

3 I enjoyed the day out even though the museum was not very interesting.

4 People travelled on horses in the past whereas today we use cars.

5 Tom watched television while he ate his tea.

6 You can't go out because you have been misbehaving.

7 I studied hard so that I would pass the exam.

8 Tom climbed the tree while the others watched him.

9 I found the treasure first therefore it's all mine!

10 Do you lock the doors whenever you are alone at home?

Objective: to use connectives to join clauses together

Name _____ Date _____

Connectives (3)

⭐ **Remember**

Connectives are **words** or **phrases** that **join clauses together** e.g. We went to school **even though** it was so foggy.

Make up some two-clause sentences of your own. Use these connectives to join the clauses in them.

because	since	however
whenever	whereas	in order to	as long as
unless	even though	so that

1 _____

2 _____

3 _____

4 _____

5 _____

6 _____

7 _____

8 _____

9 _____

10 _____

Objective: to use connectives to join clauses together

Punctuation and meaning (1)

Punctuation marks help the reader **make sense of a text**.
See what a difference punctuation marks make.
Private. No swimming allowed.
Private? No! Swimming allowed.

Copy these sentences and punctuate them correctly.
Put in the capital letters and the missing full stops,
question marks and exclamation marks.

1 the aeroplane from tokyo landed at gatwick airport

_____

2 we saw leeds united play football on saturday

_____

3 what a lovely surprise

_____

4 mrs barter is kind but mr parker is nasty to everyone

_____

5 do you prefer apples or pears

_____

6 last august we went to spain and portugal our holiday

_____

7 i absolutely hate cabbage

_____

8 roald dahl wrote charlie and the chocolate factory

_____

9 have you invited sarah to your party on Friday

_____

10 did you know that pandas are found in china

_____

Objective: to use punctuation accurately to aid the reader

Punctuation and meaning (2)

Punctuation marks help the reader **make sense of a text**.
See what a difference punctuation marks make.
Private. No swimming allowed.
Private? No! Swimming allowed.

In these sentences all the commas, apostrophes and speech marks have been left out. Copy the sentences and punctuate them correctly.

1 Mount Everest the tallest mountain in the world towered above us.

_____

2 Give me my pen Ben Louise said.

_____

3 The old car all rusty and muddy pulled up outside.

_____

4 Speaking quietly the child whispered Lets get out of here!

_____

5 Tom who looked thrilled ran to the door and shouted Ive won the lottery!

_____

6 Have you got Amys book Paul? the teacher asked.

_____

7 After a while Sam appeared and said Its time we went home.

_____

8 With a loud cry Mrs Burns exclaimed What a lovely present Peter!

_____

9 The footballers shirt which was striped was very muddy.

_____

10 Who broke Mr Turners window? the policeman asked.

_____

Objective: to use punctuation accurately to aid the reader

Punctuation and meaning (3)

Copy and punctuate each sentence correctly.

(1) snakes arent really slimy are they

_____

(2) bring me my book pencils crayons and ruler james mark said

_____

(3) sam asked how far is it to buckingham palace

_____

(4) mrs samson asked would you like to go out sarah

_____

(5) tom picked up the teachers bag the old brown bag and gave it to mr barnes

_____

(6) if you turn left youll come to hill road the man said pointing as he did so

_____

(7) the apples the ones Id just bought were rotten

_____

(8) cara who was wearing her old jeans and a T-shirt came in smiling happily

_____

(9) the thief clean shaven and long haired was arrested in sheffield

_____

(10) toms american cousin wayne boasted that he couldve eaten the whole pizza

_____

Objective: to use punctuation accurately to aid the reader

A sense of audience (1)

It is helpful to know who you are writing for (your **audience**) so that you can write in the most **appropriate style** for them. When writing for young children it is important to keep things **simple** e.g. 'I need assistance.' would be best written as 'I need help.'

Rewrite each sentence.
Choose a word from the box to replace
each underlined word to make it easier to understand.

friendly	quickly	rough	sleepy	damp
round	enough	top	rich	huge

1. The old castle was <u>colossal</u>.

   _____

2. Tom felt <u>drowsy</u> after the long walk.

   _____

3. The man reached the <u>summit</u> of the mountain.

   _____

4. The sea was very <u>tempestuous</u>.

   _____

5. Have you had <u>sufficient</u> to eat?

   _____

6. The prince was a <u>wealthy</u> man.

   _____

7. The <u>amiable</u> giant smiled at me.

   _____

8. The queen looked at herself in the <u>circular</u> mirror.

   _____

9. The girl got ready <u>promptly</u>.

   _____

10. The dog's nose was <u>moist</u>.

    _____

Objective: to understand how writing can be adapted for different audiences and purposes

A sense of audience (2)

Use a thesaurus.
Change the underlined word for a word which means the same but is harder.

(1) The dragon was <u>unbeatable</u>.

_____

(2) The black knight was an evil <u>enemy</u>.

_____

(3) The old fat frog was <u>lazy</u> and did nothing all day.

_____

(4) The boy was <u>brave</u> when he went to see the dentist.

_____

(5) It is wrong to <u>waste</u> money.

_____

(6) We are <u>lucky</u> to have such a good teacher.

_____

(7) John's face wore a <u>sad</u> expression.

_____

(8) I <u>hate</u> bad behaviour.

_____

(9) It was calm and <u>quiet</u> before the storm.

_____

(10) We can sometimes <u>shorten</u> a word by using an apostrophe.

_____

Objective: to understand how writing can be adapted for different audiences and purposes

A sense of audience (3)

Remember

It is helpful to know who you are writing for (your **audience**) so that you can write in the most **appropriate style** for them. **Official** language is often very **formal**. You find formal language on **forms**, on **notices**, in **rules** and so on e.g. Walking on the grass is prohibited.

- Play this game with a partner.
- Cut out these expressions.
- Place them face down on the table.
- Take it in turns to turn over two.
- If you turn over a formal expression and an informal expression that mean the same thing, you keep them.
- If not, turn them face down again and continue the game.
- The winner is the person at the end who has collected most formal and informal expressions.

Formal expressions	Informal expressions
Good morning.	Please sign.
Can you decipher my writing?	Get out of my way.
Kindly append your signature.	Don't eat your own food here.
I regret I am unable to attend.	Hi there.
I bid you farewell.	Sorry to have bothered you.
Please desist from walking on the grass.	Pay up right away.
Do not hinder my progress.	Can you read my writing?
Apologies for any inconvenience caused.	Cherio.
Kindly settle your debts immediately.	Keep off the grass.
Do not consume your food on these premises.	I'm sorry I can't come.

Objective: to understand how writing can be adapted for different audiences and purposes